COOKING FOR CATS

The best recipes for Felix, Orlando and the rest

Elisabeth Meyer zu Stieghorst-Kastrup
in Co-operation with
Dr. med. vet. Judith Fellinger and Marion Zerbst

DUMONT
monte

Cover photograph: zefa;
Photographs: Digital Vision pp. 4, 13 (2), 38, 40, 43; JohnFoxx p. 4; MEV p. 8;
Photo Alto pp. 4, 10/11, 13 (2); Project Photos p. 13; Annette Timmermann pp. 50/51;
Werner Waldmann pp. 4 (2), 7, 14, 15, 16, 17, 18 (2), 19 (2), 20/21, 22, 25, 26, 27, 28, 31, 32, 35, 37, 44/45, 46/47 (5), 56, 59, 60, 63, 69, 70, 75, 78, 83, 85, 86, 89, 92, 95, 99, 102, 107, 110, 117, 118, 121, 125

© 2001 DuMont Buchverlag, Köln
(Dumont monte, UK, London)

Conception and realisation: MediText, Stuttgart

Text: Elisabeth Meyer zu Stieghorst-Kastrup

Translation: Beate Gorman

Editorial supervision and design: Dr. Magda Antonic

DTP: Karolina Stuhec Meglic

Copy editing: Andrew Leslie

Food design: René Schulte

Animals: Filmtierschule Zimek

Printing: Druckerei Appl, Wemding

Printed in Germany

ISBN 3-7701-7056-3

For Tomcat Rudi

CONTENTS

Ready-made Meals 45

Tasty Dishes for Pussy 51

Amiable
Beasts of Prey

Self-willed creatures

Along with dogs, cats are humans' most popular animal companions. They were domesticated around 5,000 years ago by the Egyptians. Of course there are still plenty of wild cats that stray around, only approaching human habitation to steal something to eat or thanklessly accept a dish of food, but otherwise have no desire to live together with humans. The domestic cat, however, is a very tame animal – an affectionate, lovable house companion that demands its share of love and affection.

Anyone who owns a cat learns to love these creatures; some people even worship their pets and are absolutely crazy about them. Admittedly, this love is usually very one-sided, as cats do not love only one person the way a dog does. Cats are self-willed creatures, personalities that clearly know how to articulate their wishes.

Cats with human characteristics

Many people would say that their cats have almost human characteristics, and they are probably right when it comes to the healthy egoism prevalent among these animals. When a tomcat starts to sing to his sweetheart, it sounds like a baby crying. The cat has a remarkable talent of putting across its moods and desires in an acoustic manner. This ranges from a satisfied purring, when the animal feels contented, to an imperious meowing when it feels that it has to register its protest.

A cat's body language is even more distrinct. There is good reason why the arched back of a cat with its fur raised is a well-known signal, telling us that it is very dissatisfied. Anyone who has known their cat for a long time and knows just how to observe its actions, will understand from the interplay of expression, posture and the position of its tail and ears just what their four-legged companion wants and what it feels at that moment.

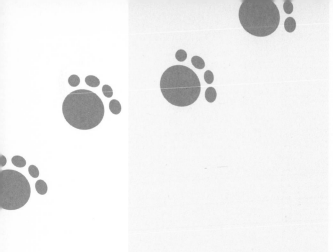

Even if they only romp around at home and have never even encountered a live mouse, cats are natural hunters. You will never be able to drive out its hunting instinct. Any little object that attracts the animal's attention soon becomes replacement quarry, and the cat then behaves instinctively as if it were hunting a mouse.

A born hunter

Two souls seem to live in the one body. When one observes a cute little cat sitting playfully on its mistress's lap purring away to its heart's content, every now and then stretching its body, the other image does not really seem to fit: namely how this cute little creature can suddenly and silently creep around the budgie's cage with the intention of attacking it. Or another scene: a very young kitten defending its bowl with an angry growl. You only have to think of the larger relatives of our domestic cat – the cats of prey living in the wild, the jaguars, tigers or lions – then you immediately realise that a dangerous animal is also slumbering in our cute little domestic cat.

Having a dog as a boarder usually does not present any problems; after all, dogs eat almost anything – especially what its master and mistress have on their plates. Of course, dogs can also be choosy and turn their nose up at certain foods. But they are in no way gourmets like cats. Cats have their own idea of what they like to eat and it is usually very difficult to get them to change their minds. It is quite common for cats that are not presented with the food that they fancy to go on a hunger strike and completely ignore the full bowl with the contempt it deserves. This can last a day, it can even last two or three days, and usually the human is the one that gives in first. After all he or she is worried about their little pet that is obviously prepared to die of hunger – although the cat would hardly let matters go that far. While these self-willed, droll, little creatures are regarded as hunger artistes, when they become hungry enough

almost any cat will be forced to accept the food that it turned its nose up at before.

Eating habits

You will never find a cat attacking its bowl and swallowing everything in one go in the same way that dogs do.

As a rule, the animal approaches the bowl very cautiously and first of all thoroughly examines the aroma. If this test is negative, the cat will quickly turn away. Perhaps it will continue to watch the bowl or have a look at its master or mistress who is observing this scene. But it will not eat.

It is obviously important to the cat that the food corresponds to its individual ideas of how an aroma should be. Considering that cats are carnivores, it is surprising that many cats do not like raw meat. As a rule, they prefer cooked meat dishes. It is also important that the food is not too dry; cats tend to enjoy food more when it is nice and juicy. Cats seldom eat everything. Therefore they are not good candidates for recycling leftovers, while a dog usually has absolutely nothing against gobbling down everything that is left on its master's plate.

Does cat food have to be attractively presented?

Anyone who is inexperienced in the ways of cats would assume that it must be enough simply to give the animal its favourite meal containing all the nutrients it needs. After all, cats are not like people who are bothered about the appearance of the food and for whom an aesthetic presentation can even enhance the appetite. Surely the same does not apply to cats!

Cats of course have no aesthetic demands regarding the presentation of their meals, but they are seldom happy to find just any old food in their bowl. It may be enough for a hungry wild cat when its bowl is filled, but the spoiled pussycat often has its specific demands, which can make it seem very human at times.

Admittedly cats have no notion of the concept of hygiene; on the other hand, they are very clean animals. There is a reason why they sit for hours licking their fur and paws. They are just as fussy when it comes to their food. They are only prepared to accept fresh food. Leftovers that have been lying in the bowl for hours on end are seldom touched later. Many cats do not like to eat if their bowl is too close to its toilet. We are no different: we also do not like sitting too close to the toilet door in a restaurant. Therefore we should show some understanding for our cat's wishes and offer it a dining area that it likes.

Playing and eating

Although eating is a serious business – after all, in the wild it makes the difference between life and death – cats find it difficult to hide their playful nature. This also applies to their eating habits. In many cases they only feel like eating while playing.

When cats are outside, you can watch how they first of all play around with a captured mouse before even considering eating the quarry. In the same way, many animals do not immediately attack their food bowl but first of all fish small titbits out of it, throw them into the air and catch them again. It is only some time later that they actually settle down and eat the food in the bowl. It is therefore understandable that cats prefer getting their nutrition in the form of appetising small titbits and balls and that a mushy mess is not very interesting to them. And if you present them with a bowl of soup or similar, it should at least look interesting and contain some tasty titbits.

Cats are not tigers. A huge pile of food is neither healthy nor appetising. You must not put too much into the cat's bowl – too much is bad for several reasons. Most cats know when they have had enough and it is seldom that a cat overeats, although dogs are often guilty of such gluttony. Cats apparently lose their appetite when the bowl is heaped too full.

Decorative food is appetising

There is nothing wrong with creating a wonderful arrangement of food for your cat; after all, both benefit from this – the human and the cat. If you look at it superficially, it might seem superfluous to arrange cat food in a decorative fashion. But why not? The cat lover gets pleasure from arranging the bowl nicely instead of just heaping the contents of a can into the bowl. You like your pet, don't you? It gives you so much pleasure – so why shouldn't you present its food in the same way that you would like it yourself? In this way you can turn the cat's feeding time into a little occasion for both of you.

Besides this, the cat will react positively to the attractive presentation of its food. When the pieces of meat, diced carrots and cat grass are arranged neatly on the plate instead of simply being mashed up together, this also appeals to the cat's heart. It can then sniff each delicacy individually – the meat, the vegetables, the grass. This is sure to be a big event for an aroma fetishist like a cat and it also increases the anticipated pleasure

of the meal. You will see that the animal sniffs at its bowl for longer than usual and only starts eating once it has finished sniffing. After all, it is much better playing with the individual bits of the meal than with an indefinable mushy mess!

So it definitely makes sense to offer your feline friend something new and special when decorating its food.

The ABC of
Cat Nutrition

Cats are not vegetarians!

Feeding cats properly demands a certain amount of knowledge, as cats do have some special requirements regarding what they can and should eat. Incorrect nourishment can very quickly lead to deficiency symptoms, which in turn can cause health problems.

In order to understand the nourishment requirements of your fluffy little green-eyed darling it is important that you know that cats are naturally carnivorous. However, their food can – and should – also contain certain vegetable ingredients. But they absolutely need meat as part of their diet. Many vegetarians who do not eat meat due to their convictions or simply because they do not like the taste of meat also want to feed their pets the same type of food. But if you do not feed your cat meat, you will harm the animal. Admittedly there are some soy sausages, nut cutlets and various other vegetarian meat replacement products on the market that look and taste so much like meat and sausages that your cat will gladly munch them down. However, if they are only served a vegetarian diet, they will slowly but surely get sick. Cats need certain nutrients that are only contained in meat.

Just like humans, they need a balanced diet, consisting of protein, fat, carbohydrates, vitamins and minerals. But cats need these building blocks in a completely different composition to humans – and dogs.

Protein – a vital part of your cat's nutrition

Protein – a vital part of your cat's nutrition. For instance, skin, hair, nails and muscles are almost pure protein. Protein is absolutely vital for the development of strong muscles. It also provides valuable calories.

Cats need meat. Vegetable nutrition alone would soon lead to serious health problems.

Every singly protein consists of long chains of individual building blocks, the so-called amino acids. Various types of proteins are formed depending on the type and sequence of these substances. The organism can produce many amino acids itself; others (the so-called essential or vital amino acids) cannot be produced by the body. These must be taken with food, otherwise there is a real danger that you or your cat will develop deficiency symptoms and illnesses.

Cats need an especially protein-rich diet. Their protein requirements are much higher than those of many other mammals, such as dogs. In particular, animal protein is vitally important for the cat, as this substance contains amino acids that the cat's organism cannot form itself. As opposed to humans, taurine and arginine are absolutely vital amino acids for your cat, and it must absorb large quantities of them with its food. Both of these amino acids are only contained in animal tissue. Arginine supports the liver in carrying out its detoxification duties; taurine is very important for the light receptors in the retina of the eye (the cones and rods). Therefore a five-week low-taurine diet – or, worse still, a completely taurine-free diet – will cause lasting damage to the retina; if the taurine deficiency continues for much longer, it can in fact lead to blindness. The most common cause of taurine deficiency in cats is feeding them with purely vegetarian food or with dog food, which has insufficient protein for cats in addition to having a deficiency of taurine.

High-protein food is the mainstay of feline nutrition.

Cats need fat

Fat is also an important nutritional constituent for cats. But the same applies here: it must be animal fat! The reason is, as proteins are made up of amino acids, fat consists of different types of fatty acids. One of these is especially important for your cat: arachidonic acid. Unilke a dog's organism, a cat cannot produce this fatty acid itself. If the cat suffers from a deficiency of this

Cats' metabolism differs from that of dogs in a quite a number of significant ways. Dog food is therefore unsuitable for cats.

substance, disorders in blood coagulation and the reproductive system can result. Arachidonic acid is only contained in animal food. If cats are fed with purely vegetarian food for long periods, they will soon suffer from an arachidonic acid deficiency.

Carbohydrates – important for the digestion

Carbohydrates (for example sugar and starch) are mainly contained in vegetable nutrition. Cats that live freely in the open eat a lot of protein and also fat, but they usually do not get enough carbohydrates, simply because they are not herbivores. Probably cats could exist without any carbohydrates – as opposed to humans, this basic foodstuff is not a vital part of the cat's diet. However, fibres are also carbohydrates. This is a group of more or less indigestible vegetable fibrous materials that are, in fact, important because they increase the stool volume and thus stimulate bowel activity. For humans, a fibre-rich diet combined with an adequate quantity of fluid intake is the best prophylactic against constipation. This also applies to cats – particularly when they do not get enough exercise. Therefore, cat food should always contain a certain proportion of fibre-rich vegetable nourishment.

Vitamins – an excess can be detrimental

Vitamins play a role in almost all important metabolic processes. Besides this, several vitamins – for example C and E – are very important for the immune system. With these vital substances, we make a distinction between water-soluble and fat-soluble vitamins. The fat-soluble vitamins (A, D, E and K) can be stored in the body and it is not absolutely essential to take these each day to cover your body's requirements. However, the water-soluble vitamins (all the B vitamins and vitamin C) must be taken regularly.

It is not a problem if one has a surplus of these water-soluble vitamins, as this excess is passed via the urine. On the other hand, many of the fat-soluble vitamins stored in the body can be hazardous to the health if they are in surplus; in some cases they can even cause poisoning. This applies, for instance, to vitamin A: high concentrations of this vitamin are found in liver. Therefore you should never feed your cat too much liver; otherwise it is could suffer from a vitamin A surplus, which in turn causes excessive bone growth and ossification of the spine. The results of this are deformation and paralysis.

Unlike humans, cats can produce vitamin C themselves. For this reason, their food should not contain large quantities of this vitamin. Most ready-made cat foods are enriched with all the vitamins that are important for your cat's health. Because of this, you should not feed your cat any vitamin preparations without first consulting your vet – especially high dosages and those containing fat-soluble vitamins. Too many vitamins will damage your cat's health rather than do it any good!

Many animals – such as cats – are able to produce vitamin C themselves. This is not the case with humans; we must be sure to consume sufficient vitamin C with our food.

Minerals

Minerals like potassium, calcium, sodium, magnesium, iron, zinc and selenium are just as important for cats as they are for humans. Calcium in particular is vital for strong teeth and hard, stable bones. However the same applies to minerals as to vitamins: they are contained in good balanced ready-made food in sufficient quantities so that if you regularly feed your cat this type of food, you will not have to feed it any additional mineral preparations.

Cat cooks require a great deal of patience

Commercially manufactured cat food also contains the right quantities of all the necessary proteins, amino acids and fatty

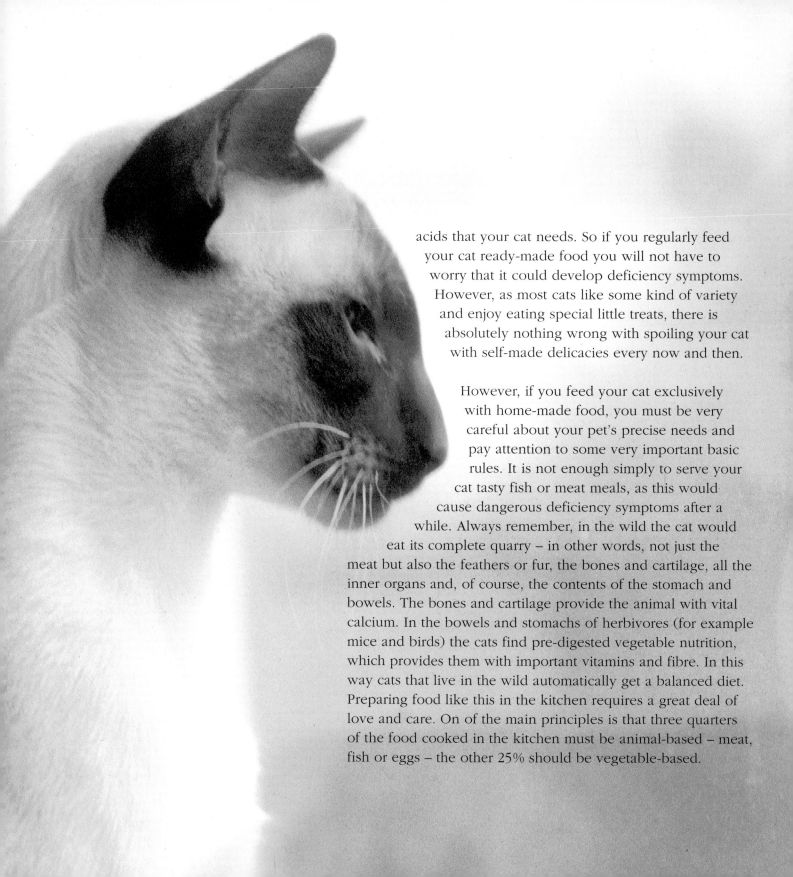

acids that your cat needs. So if you regularly feed
your cat ready-made food you will not have to
worry that it could develop deficiency symptoms.
However, as most cats like some kind of variety
and enjoy eating special little treats, there is
absolutely nothing wrong with spoiling your cat
with self-made delicacies every now and then.

However, if you feed your cat exclusively
with home-made food, you must be very
careful about your pet's precise needs and
pay attention to some very important basic
rules. It is not enough simply to serve your
cat tasty fish or meat meals, as this would
cause dangerous deficiency symptoms after a
while. Always remember, in the wild the cat would
eat its complete quarry – in other words, not just the
meat but also the feathers or fur, the bones and cartilage, all the
inner organs and, of course, the contents of the stomach and
bowels. The bones and cartilage provide the animal with vital
calcium. In the bowels and stomachs of herbivores (for example
mice and birds) the cats find pre-digested vegetable nutrition,
which provides them with important vitamins and fibre. In this
way cats that live in the wild automatically get a balanced diet.
Preparing food like this in the kitchen requires a great deal of
love and care. On of the main principles is that three quarters
of the food cooked in the kitchen must be animal-based – meat,
fish or eggs – the other 25% should be vegetable-based.

If you follow this rule you will give your cat all the roughage that it requires for a regular digestion. The best foods are rice, corn, maize meal, mashed potatoes, rolled oats and various vegetables such as carrots and broccoli. Many cats also like wholemeal pasta as a side dish. These are especially rich in valuable minerals and roughage. The vegetable-based food should always be cooked, as cats cannot utilise the starch that it contains if eaten raw.

One of the basic rules for making up a tasty and healthy menu for your cat is three quarters meat or fish and one quarter vegetable-based food.

Fish is healthy – for cats too

Because of the high proportion of protein it contains, fish is a highly valuable form of nutrition for your cat. Although most cats prefer meat, for a change you can occasionally put fish on the menu. However, it must be cooked, as raw fish contains an enzyme called thiaminasis, which cleaves and thus destroys the thiamine (vitamin B) in the cat's body. It is also important that all the bones are carefully removed from the fish – your cat could choke if it got a bone stuck in its throat. You can feed the fish skin to your cat. Tinned fish (for example tuna, mackerel or sardines) is a special treat for cats.

Fish and vegetables such as potatoes must always be cooked. Your cat cannot digest them raw.

Meat and offal

You may serve your cat beef or lamb raw; however, poultry and pork must always be cooked. It is important to remove all the bones before serving the meat to your cat, as they could splinter and injure it (especially poultry bones). The only exception is large bones that are not liable to split and which have some meat still clinging to them. When cats chew on these it keeps their teeth and gums healthy. Throat and snout meat is also good for the cat as it contains a lot of cartilage, which gives your pet something to chew on and also provides it with an extra portion of calcium. (Of course, instead of this, you can also give your cat dried meat or biscuits.)

When it comes to offal, this is where cats' tastes differ: Some cats love offal, while others do not find it quite as appetising. Most cats love liver. However, you should not feed your cat more than 100 to 200 grams per week (and this only applies to fully grown cats) otherwise there is a danger of giving your pet a surplus of vitamin A, which is detrimental to its health. Apart from this, the liver – like the kidneys – is a detoxification organ, which could be contaminated with pollutants. Kittens under a year old should not eat any liver at all.

Raw pork is another problem; it can contain the aujeszky virus, which can be deadly to cats. Pigs are the main carriers of this virus, which leads to itching and paralysis and is usually fatal. Therefore raw mixed mince (beef and pork), pig's liver and pig offal are taboo for cats.

To prevent vitamin and mineral deficiencies, you should enrich self-made food with a multi-vitamin and mineral preparation. It is especially important that your cat gets enough calcium. If you feed your cat a bone-free meat and fish diet, it is almost guaranteed to develop calcium deficiency symptoms that can lead to demineralisation. It is very important to feed kittens regular doses of calcium to ensure healthy bone development.

Every now and then, mix a finely grated carrot into your cat's food. This can prevent worms to a certain extent. Besides this, carrots contain beta-carotene – important for a strong immune system.

If you prepare your cat's food yourself, it can also develop a vitamin A deficiency if it does not get any liver or cod-liver oil: as opposed to humans, cats are unable to convert the beta carotene (the preliminary stage of vitamin A) contained in carrots and other red and green vegetables into vitamin A. A deficiency of this vitamin is just as dangerous as a surplus, as it can inhibit growth and lead to abnormal bone development. Therefore the ready-made food found in shops is almost always enriched with calcium and vitamin A.

Cats can also occasionally suffer from a thiamine (vitamin B_1) deficiency, when their owners cook for them. This can happen, for instance, if the cat is fed uncooked fish; besides this, the vitamin is very sensitive to heat – in other words, when the cat's food is cooked, thiamine is lost. (Manufacturers of ready-made food balance this out by adding thiamine to the food after it has been cooked.) Also, if the food is too one-sided, there is a danger of your cat suffering from a vitamin E deficiency. As it is virtually impossible for you to prevent all these deficiency symptoms no matter how careful you are and it is often difficult to recognise these symptoms in good time, it is vitally important that you ensure that your pet is given additional doses of all of the above-mentioned nutrients.

Multi-vitamin and mineral preparations ideally balanced to your cats' requirements are available in pet shops and other specialist outlets; read the side of the package to determine the proper dosage. You should also seek your vet's advice. He or she will be able to recommend suitable products and also provide you with some valuable nutritional tips.

If you prepare your cat's food yourself you must add vitamin and mineral preparations.

Sweets? No thanks

Cats' taste buds do not react to a sweet taste. (Dogs are different – they are quite able to distinguish the taste "sweet" and also to enjoy it because they are not such pronounced carnivores as cats.) Therefore you will not be doing your cat a favour by offering it a biscuit or a piece of chocolate. In most cases the cat is completely uninterested in such titbits and they would do the cat more harm than good, as they are very high in calories and thus ruin the cat's appetite for its normal food – without providing it with the nutrients it needs. So, if your cat sits beside the table begging for a piece of cake or a spoonful of cream – stay firm!

Much better for the cat's well-being are special cats' treats (for example crackers or chewy sticks), which you can buy in pet shops and in most good supermarkets. But the same applies again: too much is unhealthy. These little snacks in between meals should remain the exception and should not be fed in such amounts that your cat does not eat its meals.

Spicy food is also not to most cats' liking; the cat food that you prepare for your darling should only contain a little salt and no other added spices. For the same reason, you should refrain from feeding your cat scraps from the dinner table. As a rule, the food that we eat is too intensely flavoured for cats and besides, it contains too much fat and does not have sufficient nutritional value.

Why cats eat grass

Just like dogs, cats can often be seen eating grass. Occasionally they vomit after eating it. This is because cats regularly lick themselves thoroughly clean and swallow quite a lot of hair, which subsequently forms lumps in their stomach. The vegetable roughage helps them to free themselves of this ballast, by forcing them to regurgitate the matted lumps of hair.

Cats need grass. You can obtain seedling mixtures and fully-grown cat grass in trays in pet shops.

If your cat does not get outdoors very often and thus cannot eat natural grass you can buy cat grass, which is available in pet shops as seedlings in trays. (Of course, you can also buy grass or cereal mixtures and sow the grass in a tray yourself.) Make sure that your cat does not nibble at indoor plants – some plants are poisonous.

How much should a cat eat?

The same applies to cats as to humans: the amount of calories eaten should correspond to the amount of calories that the body burns up. If a cat takes in more calories than it uses, it will gradually get fat – just like most humans. (Nutritional experts describe this process as a "positive energy balance".) So, make sure your cat's energy levels are balanced out and weigh your cat regularly. If you notice that your cat is gaining weight, consult your vet. The same applies if your cat suddenly and inex-plicably loses weight - both of these conditions could be a symptom of some illness.

Another important criterion that will give you an indication of whether your cat is too fat or too thin is its ribs; you should be able to feel them but not see them. (This applies to all cats apart from very thin breeds like Siamese.)

As to just how much food your cat needs – there is no one clear answer to this, as calorie requirements vary from one cat to another and are dependent on quite a number of different fac-tors: the cat's size, its age, its condition (pregnant and suckling cats have increased calorie requirements, and the same applies to a stud cat with a very active love-life), and of course the amount of exercise it gets. Obviously cats that live indoors and

People who are out of the house from morning to night can buy feeding bowls with a time switch. These consist of a container with two removable bowls. The time switch ensures that your pet gets its food twice a day at the right time even if you are not at home.

get very little exercise need fewer calories than those who are allowed outside and are used to roaming around all night.

If you are in any doubt, your vet will be able to give you some advice and recommendations. If you feed your cat ready-made food, you can generally go by the instructions on the side of the pack or can. As a rule of thumb, an average-sized cat requires approximately 350 kilocalories per day – that corresponds to around 400 grams (almost a pound) of canned food or 200 grams (about half a pound) of fresh marbled meat. If you feed your cat poultry, you can increase this amount, as this type of meat is particularly low in calories.

Cats living in the wild eat several small meals spread throughout the day – they eat whatever they manage to catch (for example a mouse or a bird) and then go hunting again. However, you can easily get your cat used to just two meals per day – one in the morning and one again in the afternoon or evening. This is also the simplest solution for cat owners who are out at work all day. The morning meals should be a little lighter, while the second meal can be a bit richer. The important thing is that you get your cat used to regular feeding times.

Overweight – not just a problem for humans

Most cats will not eat more than they actually need, but there are some cats that overeat – especially when their master or mistress spoils them with too many tasty little titbits and treats. If, on top of this, they do not get sufficient exercise, it is a foregone conclusion that they will get fat.

You must never ignore obesity in a cat. As with humans, overweight can cause serious health problems: it burdens the limbs and can lead to diabetes and cardiovascular disorders. This why it is very important to check your cat's weight regularly.

If you find that your cat has put on a few pounds, take it to the vet. He or she will examine your cat to discover the reason for this obesity, in order to rule out any illnesses as a cause and to prepare a diet plan that will get your pet back into shape. It is very important to stick to this plan. Overweight cats are fed calorie-reduced food which ensures that the extra pounds will slowly but surely drop off: The quantity of food is reduced with each meal. Never put your cat on a crash diet – that can be hazardous to its health and can even prove fatal.

During this weight loss diet, do not feed your cat any snacks between meals. Also pay attention that no one beside yourself (for instance neighbours or children) feeds the animal or gives it titbits without your knowledge. Perhaps it will be easier for your cat to accept the reduced quantities of food if you feed it several smaller portions throughout the day instead of just twice daily – give it a try. You can also assist the weight reduction programme by encouraging your cat to move more. Play with it more often – that burns up calories, and it will also help you keep fit and slim.

What cats drink

Drinking fluids regularly is just as important for cats as it is for humans. So make sure that your cat always has a bowl of clean water available – it especially needs a lot of liquid if you feed it dry food. Ask your vet's advice if your cat does not drink enough or if it suddenly seems to be drinking more than usual – either of these could be a sign of an illness.

A little trick if your cat will not drink: Add some beef stock to the water – this makes it more appetising.

A persistent belief is that cats need milk. However, this is not founded on any nutritional basis whatsoever. On the contrary, in most cases you will not be doing your cat a favour at all by putting a saucer of milk in front of it. It will lap it up, as most cats like milk – but unfortunately cats are not able to tolerate cow's milk very well and it often gives them diarrhoea. This is because

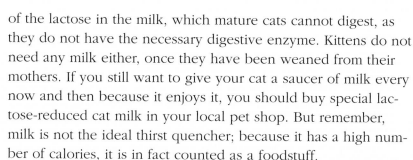

of the lactose in the milk, which mature cats cannot digest, as they do not have the necessary digestive enzyme. Kittens do not need any milk either, once they have been weaned from their mothers. If you still want to give your cat a saucer of milk every now and then because it enjoys it, you should buy special lactose-reduced cat milk in your local pet shop. But remember, milk is not the ideal thirst quencher; because it has a high number of calories, it is in fact counted as a foodstuff.

On the other hand, cats have no problems with fermented dairy products such as yoghurt, curds or cottage cheese. Most cats also really like cheese.

When cats do not want to eat

While dogs usually attack their food bowl with a great deal of enthusiasm (assuming they are healthy), cats can be rather difficult to please. A cat will not accept everything that is put in front of it; most cats would prefer to starve for a while rather than eat something that they do not like. Every animal has its own preferences, which you really should take account of. Some cats like a regular change in their diet, while others will quite happily eat the same thing day after day. Let your cat make up its own mind – if it is fed ready-made food, there is nothing wrong in feeding it the same thing every day if that is what it wants. The nutrients that it needs to remain healthy are contained in every tin of ready-made food – regardless of whether this is venison, lamb or tuna.

However, there are a few eating habits that all cats have in common and that you should pay attention to – especially if your cat is a "fussy eater":

Cats do not like cold food. They prefer their food at room temperature – after all, the mice that a cat living in the wild eats do not come from the refrigerator; they are at body temperature, which the cat finds very pleasurable while eating. So, if you keep the ready-made food for your cat in the fridge then take it out in good time and allow it to reach room temperature before offering it to your cat.

If your cat still turns its nose up at its food, warm it up to around 35 °C, or 95 °F. (Cat food should never be hotter than 40 °C, or 104 °F.) At this temperature, aromas are produced that apparently stimulate the cat's appetite. Of course, you can warm up the food in the microwave, but remember to stir it thoroughly before giving it to your cat so that it is at an even temperature throughout.

Cats are very clean animals. They do not like old dried up food that has been sitting around in their bowl for a few hours – they even dislike the smell, and it would not do them any good to eat this food as it could be infected by germs. Therefore, do not give your cat excessive portions all at once; throw away any food that is still remaining after about half an hour and regularly clean your pet's food and water bowls. This is especially important during summer or when you feed your cat tinned food.

Many cats prefer food with a high concentration of moisture. So, if your cat turns its nose up at the dry food that you offer it, try feeding it some canned food. You could also enrich the food with water or meat juices.

Cats are individualists and do not like to be watched while they are eating. Because of this, place your cat's bowl somewhere where it can eat in peace and where it is not constantly disturbed by people passing. The cat's bowl should always be in the same place – cats are creatures of habit.

Why not turn mealtimes into a game? For instance, you could hide little titbits or throw them into the garden and let your cat search for them.

The feeding bowl should be washed after every meal with hot water but without washing-up liquid.

If you have more than one cat, each should have its own food bowl. Particularly young cats have a strong sense of jealousy about food. If all the animals were to eat from the one bowl, the strongest ones would help themselves, to the disadvantage of the weaker ones. This could mean that the weaker cats do not get enough to eat or even nothing at all.

Many cats refuse to eat in times of stress – for example when moving house or if something else changes in the cat's normal environment. At times like this they require a lot of love and attention.

If your cat refuses to eat for a prolonged period, it is probably ill. The "hunger strike" can be caused by something relatively harmless like toothache or an injury in its mouth; however, your cat could have a gastrointestinal infection or it may have swallowed too much hair or some foreign matter. Take your cat to your vet so that he or she can find out the reason for your pet's sudden loss of appetite.

Family planning

Pregnant cats need more food – after all, the cat does not just have to nourish itself but also its unborn kittens. She knows this instinctively and thus begins to eat more right after mating. She will gradually increase the amount of food she eats so that in the last two weeks of the gestation period, she could be eating twice as much as usual. There is a reason for this in nature: your cat is building up reserves that she can deplete while suckling her young; she is so involved with her kittens that she does not have as much time to go hunting in the wild. Therefore, during gestation and while the animal is feeding her young you should offer her as much food as she wants. Her food should also be especially nutritious at this time.

The best thing is to buy special food for pregnant cats from your pet shop, so that the expectant mother gets everything she needs. The cat's calorie requirements are also increased while it is feeding her young – the number of calories she needs depends on the amount of milk she is producing (in other words, on the number and age of her kittens). Ensure that there is also food

available at night for the mother cat, and weigh her regularly to ensure that she is not losing weight. Only reduce the amount of food you give her once the kittens have been weaned.

During their first weeks of life, the little kittens get all the nourishment they need from their mothers' milk. This is the ideal diet for them – they do not require any additional food. The kittens will only need special replacement milk if the mother's milk is insufficient: you can obtain this from your vet. Do not feed the kittens cows' milk or goats' milk, as this will only confuse their digestive system.

When they are around two to three weeks old, the kittens begin eating solid food in addition to the mother's milk. They are only completely weaned when they are eight weeks old; by this time, they will not need any milk at all. But if you like, you can give them special cat milk: this gives them additional calcium, which is good for bone development in the little kittens.

When you offer the kittens solid food for the first time, chop it into bite-sized pieces. Ideally, dry food should be moistened. Let the kittens eat from a flat plate or a low-sided bowl. Good pet shops sell special formula kitten food, which is ideally formulated for young cats – after all, kittens have different nutritional requirements to mature animals. They also in fact need more food; so ensure that food is available for the kittens at all times. There is no danger of them overeating. Young cats should have four to five food rations of food spread throughout the day. You can start feeding the young cats food for mature animals when they are around six months old.

often does not like it and therefore (at the beginning at least) will only eat it reluctantly. How do you make it clear to a cat that is naturally used to hunting and eating meat that it has to eat low-fat and low-cholesterol food? There is only one way around this problem: trick your pet and gradually convert it very to the diet food by mixing this type of food with its normal meals and gradually increasing the proportion of diet food each day. If you are still unable to persuade your cat to end its hunger strike, it may help to warm the diet food to around 35 °C, or 95 °F.

Ready-made Meals

Cats that are fed dry food must drink a lot of water. Pay attention that the cat's water bowl is always filled with clean fresh water.

Tomcats particularly suffer from the formation of urinary calculus or gravel if they do not get enough to drink. This is because their urethra is shorter than that of a female cat.

There are so many different flavours of ready-made meals on the market these days that your cat could eat something different every day for weeks on end, if it wanted to. Besides this, ready-made food has the advantage that it is practical, saves time and provides your cat with all the nutrients it needs in the right quantities. It can also be stored for a long time and is only manufactured from high quality ingredients which are guaranteed to contain no germs.

Moist or dry food?

A distinction is made between moist or canned food (with 75 per cent moisture) and dry food such as Brekkies, which has been dehydrated so that it only contains between 12 and 15 per cent moisture. Dry food is thus more concentrated and also richer in calories than canned food, which is why you should feed it to your cat in smaller portions. You can work out how much your cat needs from the instructions on the package. Moist food has the advantage that the cat is able to cover part of its daily fluid requirements when eating it. Also, cats generally seem to prefer this to dry food. It is also a better alternative if your cat has problems with its teeth, which is often the case with older cats.

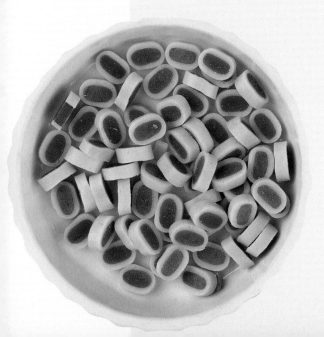

However, dry food also has some benefits: it provides the cat with something to munch on, it strengthens the gums and prevents plaque from forming on the cat's teeth. However, if your cat eats a lot of dry food, you must make sure that it drinks enough water; otherwise there is a danger of urinary calculus forming. If your cat accepts it, alternate regularly between dry and moist food.

Several manufacturers offer raw meat in practical household-sized deep freeze containers. This meat comes from certified abattoirs and is deep frozen in bite-sized pieces. As a rule, these portions are 250 or 500 grams.

You will usually find quite a broad selection including ox heart, beef, lamb, cheek meat, venison, horsemeat, salmon fillet and various mixtures of beef, heart, liver and kidneys. If you wish to save yourself the bother of cooking, you can also order deep-frozen cooked meat.

Many cat food producers also mix trace elements and minerals into the food as well as special synthetic aromas to stimulate the cat's appetite. And every cat has its own taste, so you will quite often find that an animal really enjoys the ready-made

Pay attention to the 'best by' date on dry food! If used after this date there is a danger that valuable vitamins will be lost.

food and turns its nose up at the meal that you have spent ages cooking for it. It just does not like it. Therefore you should not be too surprised, instead just let the animal have its own way.

Just the right thing for each cat's palate

It is much easier to give your cat a balanced diet using ready-made meals – therefore this is the simplest solution if you are out at work all day long or have little time for other reasons.

Specialist outlets and quite a number of supermarkets have specially prepared cat food for virtually every age and situation: ready-made food for kittens, for pregnant cats and for cats that are suckling their young, for fully grown and overweight cats and, of course, for aging cats. Read the information on the label, and you will see what you can buy to give your cat a treat and keep it healthy: many types of ready-made food contain a special oil (for example fish oil or sunflower oil) which provides your cat with a healthy glossy coat. Some foods are enriched with fibres, which stimulate digestion – ideal for animals that do not get enough exercise and thus tend to become constipated. Ready-made meals for older cats contain special high-quality protein (as older cats are no longer able to utilise protein as efficiently) and also have a higher concentration of antioxidant vitamins such as vitamins C and E, which slow down the aging process and strengthen the immune system.

Diet food has fewer calories and contains a lot of fibre, which gives your cat a pleasant feeling of being full without making it fat – this is because the cat excretes the fibre without digesting it. A high concentration of fibre is also important for long-haired cats that swallow a lot of hair when cleaning themselves and often cough up balls of hair, as fibre encourages the transport of the hair through the digestive tract, so they do not have to cough up these balls as frequently. Specialist outlets also have this type of special food for cats.

If you feed your cat canned food, buy small portions! In this way, you will not have any leftovers. Cats do not like old dried up food.

Ready-made meals for cats suffering from some form of allergy contain selected, low-allergen types of meat and are of course manufactured without colorants, preservatives, synthetic aromas or any other additives. Ready-made meals are available for cats that tend to develop urinary calculus. These meals have a reduced magnesium content. In specialist outlets, you will also find specially prepared mixtures for most other types of diseases or problems – for digestive disorders, liver and kidney disorders or diabetes, for example – so that you can give your little patient exactly what it needs.

BSE? No thanks

In these times of BSE, it is well in order to ask just how carefully commercially produced cat food is prepared. The newspapers are full of reports describing cats suffering from BSE. Of course, this dangerous bovine disease can be transferred to cats; especially at risk are big cats in zoos that are fed with raw meat. But in many ways the animals are better off than we are. While the farmers' associations and politicians were still playing down the BSE hazard, cat and dog food manufacturers reacted secretly at a very early stage. Pet food manufacturers on the continent, for instance, have not purchased any beef from the UK for the last ten years; nor do they use any other dubious tissues such as spleen, brain or spinal marrow.

If your cat tends to suffer from allergies, choose types of food without colorants, preservatives and artificial aromas.

Tasty Dishes
for Pussy

Freshly caught fillet sprinkled with cheese

- *200g/7oz haddock fillet*

- *half a cup of water*

- *a pinch of vegetable stock*

- *60g/2oz ($^1/_3$ cup) boiled rice*

- *1 Tbs oil*

- *2 Tbs Parmesan cheese, grated*

- *flat-leaf parsley as garnish*

If you don't have any Parmesan cheese, you can use Emmental instead. However, it is important that the cheese is freshly grated.

(One portion for two feline gourmets)

1. Check the fillet thoroughly for bones and remove any remaining ones.

2. Bring half a cup of water with a pinch of vegetable stock to the boil. Reduce the temperature and let the fish simmer in the liquid for approximately 20 minutes.

3. Break the haddock fillet into small pieces and mix well with the boiled rice and the oil. Let the fish-rice mixture cool down and arrange it in a stack. Sprinkle plenty of cheese onto the peak. Garnish with a sprig of parsley as a "banner".

Mackerel in a potato boat

(One portion for two feline gourmets)

1. Check the smoked fillet thoroughly for bones and remove them carefully. Mash the fish with a fork. Mash the boiled potatoes with the yoghurt to a creamy consistency.

2. Mix the mashed potatoes with the mackerel pieces and finally mix in the yeast flakes.

3. Arrange the lukewarm dish in the shape of a boat on the plate and garnish with a sprig of parsley as a "mast".

- *1 smoked mackerel fillet (approx. 200g/7oz)*
- *2 boiled potatoes*
- *2 Tbs plain yoghurt*
- *1 tsp yeast flakes*
- *flat-leaf parsley as garnish*

Note
The dish can just as easily be prepared with grilled or poached mackerel. Since mackerel can be rather fatty, this recipe should be prepared with lean fish such as plaice if your cat suffers from weight problems.

Fish risotto "Napoli" with a crown of prawns

(One portion for two feline gourmets)

- *200 g/7 oz cod fillet*
- *half a cup of water*
- *1 Tbs vegetable stock*
- *60 g/2 oz ($^1/_3$ cup) rice*
- *1–2 Tbs tomato paste*
- *6 prawns (shrimps), cooked*

Note
Cats with refined tastes like their delicacies best when they are neither too hot nor too cold. The ideal temperature is about 37 °C (100 °F).

1. Bring half a cup of water to the boil, sprinkle in the vegetable stock, bring to the boil and reduce the temperature. Let the cod fillet simmer in the hot liquid until it is cooked (remember to remove the bones beforehand). Lift the fish out carefully.

2. Slowly put the rice into the fish stock and boil to a creamy consistency while stirring vigorously. Break up the fish and mix with the rice before mixing in the tomato paste.

3. Arrange the dish once it has slightly cooled. Peel the cooked prawns (shrimps) and arrange them in the shape of a crown on top of the risotto.

Fish fricassee "Ahoy"

(One portion for two feline gourmets)

1. Cut the fish fillet into small pieces and marinade them in a mixture of salt, pepper and cider vinegar for approximately one hour.

2. Let the spinach briefly wilt in salt water, chop it up coarsely and then put it into an oven dish brushed with oil.

3. Toss the fish pieces in grated cheese and distribute evenly on top of the spinach. Whisk the milk with the egg yolk and pour the mixture over the dish, sprinkle with some grated cheese and cook in a preheated oven until the top is golden brown. Let the dish cool down a little before serving.

- *200 g/7 oz fish fillet of the cat's choice*
- *a pinch of salt*
- *a pinch of pepper*
- *1 Tbs cider vinegar*
- *80 g/3 oz ($^1/_2$ cup) spinach*
- *2 Tbs cheese, grated*
- *80 ml/2$^1/_2$ fl oz ($^1/_3$ cup) cat's milk*
- *1 egg yolk*
- *1 Tbs cheese, grated*

Swimming sardines

(One portion for two feline gourmets)

1. Heat the oil in a frying pan and mash up the sardine fillets in the oil. Add the water, stir thoroughly and bring to the boil.

2. Mix in the sliced mushrooms and let them cook for a few minutes. Finally stir the oat flakes into the soup.

- *2 tinned sardines*
- *1 Tbs oil*
- *half a cup of water*
- *1 Tbs mushrooms, finely sliced*
- *2 Tbs oat flakes*

Roulade of salmon with a creamy plaice filling

(One portion for two feline gourmets)

1. Bring the vegetables to the boil in 2 cups of salt water, reduce the temperature and let the fish fillet simmer in the liquid until it is cooked. Remove the fish and puree with a fork or a hand mixer.

2. Lay out the salmon slices, spread with the fish cream and roll them up. Tie together with sprigs of parsley.

- *1 carrot*
- *1 piece of celeriac*
- *1 piece of leek*
- *1 parsnip*
- *200 g/7 oz plaice fillet*
- *4 slices of smoked salmon*
- *flat-leaf parsley for garnish*

Tuna salad
with cheese gratin

(One portion for two feline gourmets)

• *200g/7oz tuna in oil*

• *3 Tbs sweet corn*

• *1 Tbs corn juice*

• *2 Tbs cheese, grated*

1. Mash the tuna with a fork and mix well with the sweet corn and juice from the can.

2. Arrange the salad on a plate, make a hollow with a spoon and sprinkle with grated cheese.

Tuna à la "Mimi"

(One portion for two feline gourmets)

• *200g/7oz tuna in oil*

• *2–3 anchovy fillets*

• *2 Tbs cheese, grated*

• *1 egg*

• *60g/2oz ($^1/_3$ cup) oat flakes, soaked in water*

1. Carefully mash the tuna with a fork and mix with the chopped anchovy fillets. Whisk with a fork or a hand mixer to a creamy consistency. Fold in the cheese and the egg.

2. Soak the oat flakes, squeeze out the surplus water, mix with the fish mixture and pour into a small pie dish. Allow the pie to become firm in the covered dish in a bain marie in the oven at 180°C (360°F), Gas mark 5. This takes 40–50 minutes.

Note
Cut the pie into slices and freeze them. This is a welcome snack when your feline friend gets hungry between meals.

Vegetable bake on fish

(One portion for two feline gourmets)

1. Carefully remove any remaining bones from the cod fillet. Bring 2 cups of salt water to the boil and simmer the fish in the liquid until cooked.

2. Trim the carrots and parsnip and cut into cubes. Skin the tomato, remove the seeds and cut into small pieces. Remove the cooked fish fillets from the liquid and steam the vegetables in the broth.

3. Brush an ovenproof dish with oil. Place the fish in the bottom of the dish and spread the vegetable over the fish. Whisk the eggs with the cat's milk and the grated cheese and pour over the vegetables and fish. Bake in a preheated oven for approximately 30 minutes at 180°C (360°F), Gas mark 5, until the dish is covered with a golden yellow crust. Make sure that the inside does not get too hard.

- *200g/7oz cod fillet*
- *2 carrots*
- *1 parsnip*
- *1 tomato*
- *2 eggs*
- *2 Tbs cat's milk*
- *2 Tbs cheese, grated*
- *oil for the dish*

Note
Increase the recipe quantities and prepare a delicious aspic from the broth, the pieces of fish and the vegetables. You will need 20g/²⁄₃oz of aspic.

Stuffed mackerel à la pussycat

(One portion for two feline gourmets)

- *2 mackerel fillets*
- *1 Tbs oil*
- *3–5 long macaroni*
- *100g (3½oz) ham*
- *2 Tbs boiled rice*
- *1 Tbs oat flakes, soaked in water*
- *1 Tbs tomato paste*
- *flat-leaf parsley for garnish*

1. Carefully remove any remaining bones from the fillets. Heat the oil in a frying pan and quickly fry the mackerel from all sides so that it takes on a golden brown colour. Carefully remove the fish and let it cool down.

2. Cook the macaroni al dente in salt water.

3. Cut the ham into small pieces and mix with the rice, the oat flakes soaked in water and the tomato paste.

4. Spread one fillet with the ham-rice mixture and place the other fillet on top. Carefully tie the stuffed mackerel with the macaroni. For an extra special effect, wrap a sprig of parsley around the fillets.

Note
Instead of mackerel fillets you can use any other type of firm fish such as coalfish.

Tuna balls on a bed of rice

(One portion for two feline gourmets)

- *60 g/2 oz ($^1/_3$ cup) rice*
- *200 g/7 oz tuna in oil*
- *2–3 carrots*
- *1 tsp oil or butter*
- *2–3 Tbs oat flakes, soaked in water*
- *2 Tbs Parmesan cheese*
- *1 Tbs tomato paste (optional)*
- *1 tsp cod liver oil*

1. Boil the rice al dente in salt water and put aside. Crumble the tuna into little pieces, using a fork. Trim and grate the carrots and steam in a little oil until soft. Soak the oat flakes and grate the cheese as finely as possible. Whisk one egg to a foamy consistency.

2. Mix the tuna, the grated carrots, the oat flakes, the cheese and the egg well. Alternatively, you can also fold in some extra tomato paste.

3. With moist hands, form evenly sized small balls and place them in an ovenproof dish. Set the oven to 150 °C (300 °F), Gas mark 3, and let the balls set. Put the rice on a plate and decoratively place the cooled fish balls on top. Drizzle with a little cod liver oil.

Cat bouillabaisse "Marseille"

(One portion for four feline gourmets)

1. Slice or finely dice one small onion. Peel 1–2 potatoes and cut into thin strips; trim the pepper and also cut into cubes.

2. Heat the oil in a pot, braise the vegetables for approximately 3–4 minutes; add the herbs and finally the vegetable stock.

3. Carefully remove any remaining bones from the fish, cut it into pieces and add to the broth. Then add the prawns (shrimps) and the calamari rings. Let everything simmer for approximately 10 minutes at medium temperature.

4. Remove the pot from the cooker, let the soup cool down a little and stir in the yoghurt to thicken it. Pour into 4 little bowls and decorate with a little cat grass.

- *1 small onion*
- *50 g/2 oz raw potato strips*
- *50 g/2 oz red pepper, diced*
- *1 Tbs oil*
- *1 sprig of rosemary*
- *1 sprig of thyme*
- *3 cups of vegetable stock*
- *100 g/3½ oz coalfish fillet*
- *100 g/3½ oz mackerel fillet*
- *8 prawns (shrimps)*
- *50 g/2 oz fresh calamari rings*
- *2–3 Tbs plain yoghurt*
- *cat grass*

Note
If your cat has friends over for dinner, there's one thing you should remember: friendship doesn't go so far that they will want to eat from one bowl. Serve puss and company their meals on separate plates!

Sole in a lake of aspic

- 1 tsp butter
- 200 g/7 oz sole fillet
- 2 carrots
- 30 g/1 oz mushrooms
- 1 small onion
- 2 Tbs beans, boiled (can)
- 20 g/$\frac{2}{3}$ oz aspic powder

Note
If your little tiger doesn't like green beans and prefers zucchini (courgette) instead, simply exchange the vegetables.

(One portion for two feline gourmets)

1. Carefully remove any remaining bones from the fillet. Heat the butter in a frying pan and fry the fillet from both sides until golden brown. Remove the cooked fish and put aside.

2. Trim and slice the carrots and mushrooms and finely dice a small onion. Steam the vegetables in the fish pan and add some more butter if necessary. Try not to mix the vegetables. Heat the green beans in a pot.

3. Place the fried sole fillet in an oval or round dish. Distribute the vegetables with a spoon in little heaps around the fish, arranged according to colour, and let everything cool down a little.

4. Bring 2 cups of water to the boil, stir in the aspic and stir vigorously. Cover the fish and vegetables with the liquid mixture. Allow the mixture to set and serve as a whole or in portions.

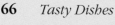

Rolled up plaice in a lifeboat

(One portion for two feline gourmets)

1. Carefully remove any remaining bones from the plaice fillets. Heat the butter in a frying pan and fry the fillets for 2–3 minutes.

2. Trim and grate the carrots and steam them in a little water. Soak the oatmeal in water. Mix the carrots, sour cream, oatmeal and yeast flakes well. Spread the mixture on to the fillets and roll them up carefully so that they don't fall apart.

3. Bring 2 cups of water to the boil, stir in the aspic and stir vigorously. Put the rolled up plaice fillets one by one in a small, preferably oval pie dish. Pour the liquid aspic around the sides of the dish without covering the fish.

4. Once the aspic has set, turn the tureen upside down onto a plate. On each side, press 3 large peeled prawns (shrimps) into the aspic as "oars".

- *200 g/7 oz plaice fillet*
- *1 Tbs butter or oil*
- *3 small carrots*
- *1 Tbs sour cream*
- *3 Tbs oatmeal*
- *1 Tbs yeast flakes*
- *20 g/²⁄₃ oz aspic*
- *6 prawns (shrimps)*

Note
Instead of aspic, these delicious plaice rolls could also sail on a "lake" of vegetables such as carrots and peas.

Salmon mousse on potato fritters

(One portion for two feline gourmets)

- ½ tsp vegetable stock
- ⅓ cup of water
- 100 g/3½ oz salmon fillet
- 2 Tbs cat's milk
- 1 Tbs plain yoghurt
- 2 raw potatoes
- ½ onion
- a pinch of salt
- a pinch of nutmeg, grated
- 2–3 Tbs oil
- 1 Tbs boiled peas (can)

1. Cook the salmon in a little vegetable stock, remove from the pot and allow to cool. Whisk the fish with the cat's milk and the plain yoghurt to a creamy consistency with a fork or hand mixer.

2. Peal and grate the potatoes and grate the onion. Whisk an egg, mix well with the grated potatoes and onion and season with salt and grated nutmeg.

3. Heat the oil in a frying pan, shape small flat pancakes with moist hands or spoons and fry these pancakes from both sides to a golden brown colour at a moderate temperature, turning them several times.

4. Let the cooked potato fritters cool down a little and arrange on a plate while still lukewarm. Fill the salmon mousse into an icing bag and make a crown of mousse on the pancakes. You could additionally decorate the crown with boiled peas as "gemstones".

Note
If your cat has a sweet tooth, you could serve creamy apple sauce with sugar and cinnamon with the crispy potato fritters instead of the salty salmon foam.

"North Sea waves" ocean perch roulades

- 200g/7oz ocean perch fillets
- a pinch of salt
- 1 Tbs lemon juice
- 4 smoked anchovy fillets
- $\frac{1}{2}$ tsp soy sauce
- $\frac{1}{2}$ tsp lemon juice
- 2 carrots
- 1 small spring onion
- 40g/1$\frac{1}{2}$oz North Sea prawns (shrimps)
- 1 Tbs oil
- 100ml ($\frac{1}{2}$ cup) vegetable stock
- 100g/3$\frac{1}{2}$oz ($\frac{2}{3}$ cup) boiled rice

Note
If you add more vegetable stock, you can bring the fish stock to the boil with aspic, let the stock cool down, pour into a dish and allow to set overnight. Cut into cubes and serve to your cat as a tasty snack in between meals.

(One portion for two feline gourmets)

1. Carefully remove any remaining bones from the fillets, salt the fillets and drizzle with lemon juice. Using a fork, mash the anchovy fillets with soy sauce and a little lemon juice to a creamy consistency. Spread the mixture onto the ocean perch.

2. Trim the carrots and cut into fine strips; cut the spring onion into fine rings. Spread the vegetables with the North Sea prawns (shrimps) onto the fillets. Roll up the roulades and fasten with toothpicks or tie together with string.

3. Heat the oil in a frying pan and carefully fry the roulades from all sides. Add the vegetable stock, reduce the temperature and simmer the roulades for 10 to 15 minutes.

4. Remove the roulades from the frying pan, let them cool down a little and cut into slices. Arrange the boiled rice in the shape of waves on a plate and place the roulade slices in a "trough".

Fresh and fine fish fillet

(One portion for two feline gourmets)

1. Trim the fillets and, if necessary, carefully remove any remaining bones with tweezers. Drizzle lemon juice onto both sides of the fish and season with salt. Then toss the fillets in flour.

2. Finely dice the onion, trim and chop the chanterelles and chop the parsley.

3. Heat the butter or oil in the frying pan and fry the fish briefly on both sides. Remove and put aside.

4. Add the onion, chanterelles and herbs to the butter and briefly fry while stirring constantly. Add the water and sour cream, place the fish fillets in the frying pan again and simmer for approximately another 10 minutes.

5. Let the fish cool down a little, break into coarse pieces, arrange in the cat's bowl and spoon the chanterelle cream sauce over it.

- *200 g/7 oz plaice fillets*
- *1 Tbs lemon juice*
- *a pinch of salt*
- *1 Tbs flour*
- *½ onion*
- *50 g/2 oz chanterelles*
- *a few sprigs of flat parsley*
- *1 Tbs flour*
- *1 Tbs water*
- *2 Tbs sour cream*

Note
If there is no fishmonger's near you, you could use deep-frozen fillets.

Tuna on a bed of vegetables

(One portion for two feline gourmets)

1. Finely dice the shallots, chop the garlic, trim the red and green peppers and cut into short, thin strips.

2. Dip the tomatoes into boiling water, make notches at the top to skin them, remove the seeds and cut into pieces.

3. Salt the tuna, drizzle with lemon juice and place in the fridge for a short while.

4. Heat the oil in a frying pan and sauté the vegetables. Place the fish on top, stir in the tomato paste after approximately 5 minutes and add the vegetable stock. Cover the frying pan and simmer at a moderate temperature for another 15 minutes. Remove the fish and put aside.

5. Thicken the vegetables with the oat flakes and sprinkle with the chopped sage and parsley. Allow to cool down a little and place in the cat's bowl. Break the tuna into pieces and place on top of the vegetables.

- *2 shallots*
- *1 garlic clove*
- *$\frac{1}{2}$ red pepper*
- *$\frac{1}{2}$ green pepper*
- *2 tomatoes*
- *200 g/7 oz fresh tuna*
- *a pinch of salt*
- *1 Tbs lemon juice*
- *2 Tbs oil*
- *1 Tbs tomato paste*
- *$\frac{1}{2}$ cup vegetable stock*
- *1–2 Tbs oat flakes*
- *2 sage leaves*
- *2 flat-leaf parsley leaves*

Chicken in a mackerel jacket

(One portion for two feline gourmets)

- 50 g/2 oz smoked mackerel
- 2 Tbs oat flakes
- 1 Tbs yeast flakes
- 1 egg
- 100 g/3½ oz chicken meat
- 1 Tbs oil

1. Place the mackerel in a bowl. Add the oat, yeast flakes and egg and blend with the hand mixer to a form spreadable paste.

2. Cut the chicken meat into cubes and spread with the cream. Heat the oil in a frying pan and fry the meat from all sides until it is well cooked. Let the meat cool down, decorate with a parsley leaf and garnish with a dot of tomato paste.

Roast hare à la pussycat

(One portion for two feline gourmets)

- 100 g/3½ oz hare fillet
- 1 Tbs oil
- 3–4 prunes, soaked in water
- 1 Tbs redcurrant jelly
- ½ Tbs flour
- 1 Tbs cider vinegar
- cat grass or parsley for garnish

1. Cut the hare fillet into pieces. Heat the oil in the frying pan and quickly fry the meat from all sides. Add the soaked, finely chopped prunes, stir in the redcurrant jelly and flour and add the cider vinegar. Let everything simmer for approximately 15 minutes.

2. Let the mixture cool a little and arrange in the shape of a hare on a plate. Make eyes, teeth, whiskers and tail from cat grass or parsley.

Vegetable soup with morsels of beef

(One portion for two feline gourmets)

1. Bring the water to the boil and stir in the vegetable stock. Cut the beef into bite-sized pieces and add to the stock.

2. Trim the carrot and cut into slices, peel and dice the potato and the celeriac and cut the leek into rings. Put everything into the stock and simmer together with the meat for approximately 30–40 minutes. Finally mix in the vinegar and the oat flakes. Allow the broth to cool down a little, pour into a bowl and decorate with some sprigs of flat-leaf parsley.

- *1 tsp vegetable stock*
- *1 cup of water*
- *150g/5oz beef*
- *1 carrot*
- *1 potato*
- *1 piece of celeriac*
- *1 piece of leek*
- *1 tsp cider vinegar*
- *2 Tbs oat flakes*

Birthday roast for the cat

(One portion for two feline gourmets)

- *150 g/5 oz beef fillet*
- *a pinch of salt*
- *a pinch of pepper*
- *1 slice of ham*
- *1 slice of streaky bacon*
- *1 Tbs butter*
- *$1/2$ cup vegetable stock*
- *2 Tbs sour cream*
- *1 tomato*
- *1 onion*
- *1 carrot*
- *1 piece of celeriac*
- *60 g/2 oz mushrooms*
- *60 g/2 oz boiled rice*

1. Season the beef fillet with salt and pepper. Place the ham and bacon on top of the meat slice and tie with string.

2. Heat the butter in a frying pan and brown the fillet on both sides. Add the vegetable stock and sour cream, reduce the temperature and cook the meat with the quartered tomato, diced onion, carrot slices, finely chopped celeriac and lemon rind for approximately 20 minutes.

3. Remove the meat and lemon rind. Add the mushroom slices to the vegetables in the frying pan and simmer briefly.

4. Remove the string from the meat and allow the meat to settle for a while. Add the boiled pasta to the vegetables in the frying pan and mix. Arrange the pasta and vegetables in pussy's favourite bowl and place the fillet cut into bite-sized pieces on top.

Pussy burger
for little tigers

(One portion for two feline gourmets)

- 100 g/3½ oz minced beef
- 2 Tbs oat flakes, soaked in water
- 1 tsp yeast flakes
- 1 egg, beaten
- 1 Tbs oil
- ½ beef tomato
- some fresh or pickled cucumber slices
- 1–2 Tbs tomato paste
- a little cat grass

1. Mix the minced beef with the oat flakes soaked in water, the yeast flakes and the beaten egg and shape small flat patties. Heat the oil in a frying pan and fry the patties on both sides. Remove and put aside.

2. Carefully roast the tomato slices in the frying pan, so that they do not fall apart. Place one slice on a plate and arrange the cucumber slices and the meat patty on top. Add some more cucumber on top of the burger and then another slice of tomato. Make a little mouse from tomato paste next to the cat burger and a little ball from cat grass.

Note
Cats need grass to aid their digestion, so that they can regurgitate the hairs which they swallow when grooming themselves. Special cat grass is available in pet shops.

Beef aspic à la Felix

(One portion for two feline gourmets)

1. Bring 2 cups of water to the boil and add the vegetable stock. Place the beef in the water, reduce the heat and allow the meat to simmer for approximately 20 minutes.

2. Trim and dice the carrot, the parsnip and the red pepper, finely dice the onion and slice the mushrooms. Put everything into the soup and boil. Finally add the peas.

3. Remove the meat and chop it up, then ladle the vegetables into a bowl.

4. Bring the stock to the boil and stir in the aspic. Arrange the meat and vegetables decoratively in a dish. Pour the aspic stock over the meat and vegetables and allow to set.

- *1 tsp vegetable stock*
- *100 g (3½ oz) beef*
- *1 carrot*
- *1 parsnip*
- *½ red pepper*
- *1 small onion*
- *30 g/1 oz mushrooms*
- *2 Tbs peas (can)*
- *20 g/⅔ oz aspic powder*

Note
You can also turn the aspic onto a plate: briefly put the bowl into hot water until the aspic loosens from the sides. It can then be turned onto a platter.

Cat baseballs

- *80 g/3 oz ($^1/_2$ cup) rice*
- *1 carrot*
- *1 egg*
- *1 tsp oil*
- *100 g/3$^1/_2$ oz minced beef*
- *80 g/3 oz ($^1/_2$ cup) oat flakes*

Note
Cats are easily tempted to play. Of course, it is double the fun when the exciting balls can also be eaten!

(One portion for one feline gourmet)

1. Boil the rice al dente in a little salt water and put into a bowl. Trim and grate the carrot and fold into the rice with the egg and the olive oil. Finally add the minced beef.

2. Knead the ingredients thoroughly with moist hands and shape into little balls. Pour the oat flakes onto a plate and roll the balls in the flakes.

Extra-special meat burger

- 100 g/3¹⁄₂ oz minced beef
- 60 g/2 oz smoked salmon
- 2 carrots
- ¹⁄₂ onion
- 1 egg
- 1 tsp cider vinegar
- 2 Tbs vegetable stock
- 2 Tbs oat flakes
- 1 Tbs oil
- 40 g/1¹⁄₂ oz (¹⁄₃ cup) Emmental cheese, grated

(One meal for two feline gourmets)

1. Mix the minced beef with the finely chopped smoked salmon.

2. Grate the carrots and the onion half and add to the beef-fish mixture, then add the beaten egg, the cider vinegar and the chicken stock. Finally mix everything well together with the oat flakes.

3. Shape 4 small flat patties with moist hands. Heat the oil in a frying pan and fry the burgers briefly on both sides.

4. Sprinkle a generous amount of cheese on the patties. Preheat the grill in the oven and leave the meat burgers in, until the cheese has melted and has a light golden brown colour.

Note
You don't always have to use minced beef. If your cat likes lamb, simply replace the beef mince in the recipe with lamb mince.

Fiery heart "Viva México"

(One portion for two feline gourmets)

1. Chop or shred the ox heart into small pieces.

2. Trim the red and green peppers and cut into thin strips; finely dice the onion.

3. Heat the oil in a frying pan and stir-fry the vegetables. Add the ox heart and gradually fry the mixture. Season with salt and coarsely ground pepper and add the cider vinegar.

4. Fill into a bowl and mix with the sweet corn and the grated cheese. Sprinkle with the green and black olives cut into thin rings.

- *60 g/2 oz ox heart*
- *½ red pepper*
- *½ green pepper*
- *1 small onion*
- *1 Tbs oil*
- *a pinch of salt*
- *coarsely ground pepper*
- *1 tsp cider vinegar*
- *2 Tbs sweet corn (can)*
- *1 Tbs cheese, grated*
- *4 pitted green olives*
- *4 pitted black olives*

Note
As a side dish for spicy dishes serve a creamy, slightly nutty but not too sweet avocado cream. Mash the meat with a little sour cream, lemon juice and salt to a creamy consistency with a fork or a hand blender.

Broken heart in a bowl

(One meal for four feline gourmets)

1. Heat the water and stir in the vegetable stock. Cut the ox heart and the pig's heart into bite-sized pieces and simmer in the slowly boiling stock for several minutes. Remove and put aside.

2. Bring the stock to the boil again. Dip the tomato into the hot liquid, remove, notch the top and remove the skin. Seed and finely dice the tomato. Trim and grate the carrot and peel and grate the cucumber.

3. Soak the oat flakes in some stock and dice the slice of bacon.

4. Put the cooked heart into a bowl, add the tomato pieces, the grated carrot and cucumber, the oat flakes and the bacon and mix well. Coarsely mash with a fork.

5. Arrange in a dish, sprinkle with Parmesan cheese and garnish with the chopped herb mixture consisting of parsley, chives and basil.

- *2 cups of water*
- *1 Tbs vegetable stock*
- *100 g/3½ oz ox heart*
- *100 g/3½ oz pig's heart*
- *1 medium-sized tomato*
- *1 carrot*
- *1 piece of cucumber*
- *3 Tbs oat flakes*
- *1 rather thick slice of bacon*
- *1 Tbs Parmesan cheese, grated*
- *some parsley, chives and basil*

Note
Put your cat's favourite vegetables (finely chopped) into the nourishing heart stock, bring to the boil and stir in approximately 10 g/⅓ oz of aspic. Let the aspic set, cut into cubes and serve as a side dish or a tasty snack in between meals.

Cold heart in aspic

(One meal for four feline gourmets)

- *300 g/10 oz ox heart*
- *1 carrot*
- *1 parsnip*
- *1 piece of celeriac*
- *$\frac{1}{2}$ red pepper*
- *1 potato*
- *1 piece of zucchini (courgette)*
- *4 cups of water*
- *2 Tbs vegetable stock*
- *40 g/1$\frac{1}{2}$ oz ($\frac{1}{4}$ cup) rice*
- *40 g (1$\frac{1}{2}$ oz) aspic powder*

Note
You can also serve the dish as a "warm heart" in the bowl, if the ingredients are served in the nourishing stock. In this case, however, you should stir in some oat flakes to thicken the mixture.

1. Chop or shred the ox heart into little pieces. Trim and slice the carrot and the parsnip. Dice the celeriac, the red pepper, the potato and the zucchini (courgette).

2. Bring the water to the boil and sprinkle into the vegetable stock. Put all ingredients into the stock, add the rice and simmer for approximately 20 minutes at a moderate temperature.

3. Strain the liquid through a sieve and arrange the meat and vegetables in a heart-shaped dish.

4. Bring the stock to the boil, stir in the aspic powder and allow the mixture to cool slightly. Pour into the dish and let it set for several hours.

Tasty liver pieces with potato mousse

(One portion for four feline gourmets)

- 100g/3½oz calf's liver
- 3 Tbs oat flakes, soaked in water
- 1 Tbs parsley, chopped
- 1 egg
- 4 potatoes, boiled in their skin
- a pinch of salt
- 1 Tbs butter
- ½ cup of milk
- 2 cups of water
- 1 Tbs vegetable stock
- flat-leaf parsley for garnish

1. Chop the raw calf's liver and thoroughly mix the soaked oat flakes, the chopped parsley and the egg. Shape small balls with moist hands, put into a cool place and allow to dry slightly.

2. In the meantime, peel the potatoes that have been boiled in their skin, season with salt, mash with a little butter and whisk with hot milk to a creamy consistency.

3. Bring the water to the boil, sprinkle in the vegetable stock and reduce the temperature. Gradually cook the liver dumplings in the slowly simmering liquid, remove and let them cool down.

4. Put little heaps of potato snow on a plate and decorate each with a tasty liver dumpling. Garnish with parsley leaves.

Note
If your cat appears not to crave potato dishes, why not try rice instead.

Chicken liver and onion mix

(One portion for two feline gourmets)

1. Finely cut the chicken liver and slice the onion into thin rings. Core the apple and cut into slices.

2. Heat the oil in a frying pan and slowly fry the liver along with the onion rings. Finally add the apple slices and briefly boil.

3. Add the cider vinegar to the meat juices, then add the honey and mix well. Let the mixture cool down a little and round it off with the plain yoghurt.

4. Arrange the liver with the onion rings and the apple slices on a plate and garnish with some dots of redcurrant jelly.

- *100 g/3$\frac{1}{2}$ oz chicken liver*
- *1 small onion*
- *1 small sweet apple*
- *1 Tbs oil*
- *1 Tbs cider vinegar*
- *$\frac{1}{2}$ tsp honey*
- *2 Tbs plain yoghurt*
- *redcurrant jelly for garnish*

Red heart à la Felicity

(One portion for two feline gourmets)

- *60 g/2 oz ox heart*
- *1 small carrot*
- *1 piece of zucchini (courgette)*
- *4 beetroot slices*
- *¹/₂ tomato*
- *1 Tbs cider vinegar*
- *1 tsp sour cream*
- *cat grass or fresh herbs for garnish*

1. Finely shred the ox heart. Trim and coarsely grate the carrot and zucchini (courgette), dice the cooked beetroot slices and the tomato.

2. Heat the oil in a frying pan, fry the finely shredded heart on all sides, add the vegetables and let everything cook for several minutes.

3. Add the beetroot juice and the cider vinegar, allow the mixture to cool down a little and stir in some sour cream to round off.

4. Arrange three red hearts on a white plate and garnish with cat grass or fresh herbs.

Note

If your cat prefers kidney, you can easily modify this recipe. There is only one difference: soak the kidney for several hours in milk before cooking.

Tripe for Tigger

(One portion for two feline gourmets)

- 60 g/2 oz boiled tripe

- 30 g/1 oz streaky bacon

- ½ onion

- 1 Tbs butter

- a few rosemary leaves

- half a cup of vegetable stock

- 2–3 Tbs oat flakes

- 2 Tbs Parmesan cheese, grated

1. Cut the boiled tripe into strips. Dice the onion and the bacon.

2. Heat the butter in a pot and brown the bacon and onion cubes while constantly stirring.

3. Add the strips of tripe and the rosemary and pour in the vegetable stock. Place the lid on the pot and simmer everything at a low temperature for approximately 30 minutes.

4. Remove the tripe, reduce the liquid a little and thicken with oat flakes.

5. Put the tripe into the bowl and pour the thickened stock over it. Sprinkle with plenty of Parmesan cheese.

Note
Blanche the tripe beforehand so that it takes on a nice white colour. Cut into strips or chunks.

Toadstool hearts

(One portion for two feline gourmets)

1. Bring the water to the boil and sprinkle in the vegetable stock. Put the chicken hearts into the liquid either whole or chopped and cook for a few minutes. Remove and put aside.

2. Stir the tomato paste into the stock and sprinkle in the chopped parsley.

3. Arrange the chicken hearts in a bowl and pour the tomato soup over them. With a small spoon, scoop out some sour cream and distribute this as white "toadstool dots" on top of the red soup.

- *1 cup of water*
- *1 tsp vegetable stock*
- *100 g/3½ oz chicken hearts*
- *3 Tbs tomato paste*
- *1 Tbs parsley, chopped*
- *1 Tbs sour cream*

Steak tatar "Chat surprise"

(One portion for two feline gourmets)

1. Mix the minced fillet steak with the other ingredients. With moist hands shape flat patties from the boiled rice and the oat flakes, soaked in water. Place the steak tatar on top.

2. Arrange on a plate and garnish, e.g. with sweet corn and olives, anchovies and capers, chopped chives and onion pieces or with grated cheese and parsley.

- *60 g/2 oz minced fillet steak*
- *salt and pepper*
- *½ onion, diced*
- *60 g/2 oz (⅓ cup) boiled rice*
- *60 g/2 oz (⅓ cup) oat flakes, soaked in water*
- *sweet corn, olives, anchovies, capers, chopped chives, grated cheese and parsley for garnish*

"Miaow" roulade

(One portion for four feline gourmets)

1. Roll out the meat. Mix the tomato paste with a little mustard and spread on the roulade. Place a slice of streaky bacon on top of the meat.

2. Trim and slice the mushrooms and finely dice the onion. Heat the butter in the frying pan, brown the mushrooms and the onion, until the onion takes on a golden yellow colour, then season with a pinch of salt and pepper. Add the cider vinegar and stir in the parsley. Let the mixture cool.

3. Spread the filling on top of the meat and roll it up. Tie up with string like a parcel and knot the ends.

4. Heat the oil in a pot, seal the meat on all sides and remove from the pot.

5. To make the sauce, brown the diced carrot and onion in butter and add the tomato paste and vegetable stock. Briefly bring to the boil and reduce a little. Add the roulade and simmer in the covered pot at a moderate temperature for approximately 30 minutes.

6. Remove the string, cut the beef olive into slices and serve with the sauce, thickened with soaked oat flakes.

- *200 g/7 oz beef roulade*
- *1 Tbs tomato paste*
- *$\frac{1}{2}$ tsp mustard*
- *1 slice of streaky bacon*
- *30 g/1 oz mushrooms*
- *1 small onion*
- *1 Tbs butter*
- *a pinch of salt and pepper*
- *1 Tbs cider vinegar*
- *1 Tbs parsley, chopped*
- *string*
- *2 Tbs oil*
- *1 Tbs butter*
- *$\frac{1}{4}$ cup carrots, diced*
- *$\frac{1}{4}$ cup onion, diced*
- *1–2 Tbs tomato paste*
- *$\frac{1}{2}$ cup vegetable stock*
- *3 Tbs oat flakes, soaked in water*

"Hungry cat" stew

(One portion for four feline gourmets)

- 400 g/14 oz beef
- 1 bouquet garni
- 150 g/5 oz shell-shaped pasta
- 3 carrots
- 40 g/1½ oz (¼ cup) peas
- 100 g/3½ oz (½ cup) green beans
- chives and parsley

1. Put the beef and bouquet garni into boiling water and simmer for approximately 90 minutes at a low temperature.

2. Remove the bouquet garni and add the paste. After another 20 minutes add the diced carrots, peas and beans to the soup. Simmer for another hour.

3. Remove the beef and cut into bite-sized pieces and also chop the vegetables of the bouquet garni.

4. Place some liquid and plenty of pasta and vegetables into the bowl. Place the meat on top and cover with the herbs and vegetables from the bouquet garni. Sprinkle with chopped herbs such as chives and parsley.

Beetroot risotto

(One portion for two feline gourmets)

1. Peel the beetroot, dice and cook in a little salt water. Cut the broccoli into small florets and skin, seed and finely chop the tomato.

2. Cut the ham or chicken into bite-sized pieces and put aside. Bring the water to the boil and stir in the vegetable stock.

3. Heat the oil in a frying pan, brown the rice and add some vegetable stock. Stirring vigorously, pour in more stock and mix thoroughly. Repeat this process until all the stock has been soaked up and the rice has a creamy consistency. Add the broccoli and tomato and simmer for a few more minutes.

4. Let the risotto cool down a little and mix in the beetroot cubes and the shredded meat. Put into a bowl and garnish with some cat grass or parsley leaves.

- *1 beetroot*
- *30 g/1 oz broccoli*
- *1 small tomato*
- *80 g/3 oz ham or cooked poultry*
- *half a cup of water*
- *$\frac{1}{2}$ tsp instant vegetable stock*
- *1 Tbs oil*
- *60 g/2 oz ($\frac{1}{3}$ cup) rice*
- *cat grass or flat-leaf parsley*

Note
Since it takes almost an hour to cook the beetroot, it is advisable to use the pressure cooker. In many supermarkets you can buy prepared shrink-wrapped beetroot.

Paella "Viva España"

(One portion for four feline gourmets)

- 1 onion
- 1 red pepper
- 1 green pepper
- 3–4 Tbs oil
- 60 g/2 oz ($^1/_3$ cup) rice
- 2 Tbs tomato paste
- a pinch of salt
- pepper
- a pinch of saffron
- 1 cup of chicken stock
- 2 Tbs oil
- 100 g/3$^1/_2$ oz rabbit
- 150 g/5 oz chicken
- 60 g/2 oz ($^1/_3$ cup) peas
- 6 prawns (shrimps), boiled
- 4 pitted green olives
- 4 pitted black olives

1. Dice the onion and cut the red and green pepper into thin strips.

2. Heat the oil in a frying pan, brown the onion and pepper, stir in the rice and tomato paste and season with salt, pepper and a pinch of saffron. Fill up with the chicken stock. Let the mixture simmer for 20 minutes until the rice is boiled.

3. Heat oil in a pot and cook the chopped rabbit meat at a low temperature for approximately 15 minutes, turning the meat constantly.

4. Chop the boiled chicken meat into bite-sized pieces and mix into the rice together with the peas and rabbit meat. Let everything simmer for another few minutes at a low temperature.

5. Once the dish has cooled down a little, place on a plate and garnish with the peeled prawns (shrimps) and sliced olives.

Chicken breast fillet au naturel

- 60g/2oz ($^1/_3$ cup) rice
- 2 Tbs oil
- 300g/10oz chicken breast fillet (put aside 100g/3$^1/_2$oz for the balls)
- 1 tsp cider vinegar
- 1–2 Tbs vegetable stock
- 1 Tbs yeast flakes
- 60g/2oz ($^1/_3$ cup) peas and carrots (can)

1. Bring the salt water to the boil, sprinkle in the rice, simmer and let the rice swell up.

2. Heat the oil in a frying pan and carefully fry the chicken breast fillet on both sides. Reduce the temperature, add the cider vinegar and the stock, cover and simmer for approximately 30 minutes.

3. Remove the meat and put aside. Stir the yeast flakes into the liquid.

4. Heat the peas and carrots and then mix with the rice. Cut the meat into bite-sized pieces and serve with the rice-vegetable mixture. Finally drizzle with the jus.

Chicken balls "Cock-a-doodle-doo"

- 60g/2oz ($^1/_3$ cup) oat flakes, soaked in water
- 1 egg
- 1 tsp oil
- 2 Tbs parsley, chopped

(One portion for two feline gourmets)

1. Thoroughly mix the oat flakes soaked in water with the egg, oil and finely chopped and steamed chicken meat.

2. Shape little balls with moist hands and roll in the chopped parsley.

Cat's feast Provençal

(One portion for four feline gourmets)

1. If necessary, remove fat from beef and cut into bite-sized pieces.

2. Peel and dice the onion. Peel and crush the garlic cloves. Seed the tomatoes and cut into quarters, trim and seed the red and green peppers and cut into rings. Thinly slice the zucchini (courgette) and the eggplant.

3. Heat the oil in a pot and fry the onion and garlic. Then add the tomatoes and the remaining vegetables one by one. Add a little tomato juice and season with herbes de provençe.

4. Heat a little oil in a frying pan and brown the meat on all sides while stirring constantly.

5. Add the meat to the ratatouille in the pot and simmer at a low temperature for approximately 20 minutes. Finally, thicken the vegetable liquid with oat flakes if necessary.

6. Let the dish cool down slightly and serve in the cat's bowl. Sprinkle with freshly chopped herbs for garnish.

- *200 g/7 oz beef*
- *1 onion*
- *2 garlic cloves*
- *1 beef tomato*
- *1 red pepper*
- *1 green pepper*
- *1 small zucchini (courgette)*
- *1 piece of eggplant*
- *2 Tbs oil*
- *half a cup of tomato juice*
- *1 tsp herbes de provençe*
- *1 Tbs oil*
- *oat flakes for thickening (optional)*
- *fresh herbs such as rosemary, thyme, basil, parsley*

Note
If you want to spoil your cat with this dish at Easter, you could use lamb instead of beef.

Chicken in a nest

(One portion for two feline gourmets)

1. Shred the chicken meat such as a breast fillet. Cut the streaky bacon into cubes.

2. Finely chop the onion and trim and cut the mushrooms into small pieces.

3. Bring the salt water to the boil and sprinkle in the rice. Let it come to the boil again, reduce the heat and let the rice swell up in approximately 20 minutes.

4. Heat the streaky bacon with a little butter in the frying pan. Fry the bacon until it becomes transparent and then add the onions. Add the meat and stir-fry. Finally mix in the mushrooms and add the cider vinegar.

5. Reduce the heat, pour in the vegetable stock and simmer for approximately 20 minutes. Let the mixture cool down a little and round off with the sour cream.

6. Shape little nests from the boiled rice, put on a plate and fill with the shredded chicken. Garnish each nest with some sprigs of parsley.

- *200 g/7 oz chicken breast fillet*
- *1 thick slice of streaky bacon*
- *1 onion*
- *60 g/2 oz brown mushrooms*
- *100 g/3 1/2 oz (2/3 cup) rice*
- *1 tsp butter*
- *1 Tbs cider vinegar*
- *2 Tbs vegetable stock*
- *2 Tbs sour cream*
- *flat-leaf parsley for garnish*

Note
If your cat is a real gourmet, prepare the dish with cep mushrooms, which give it that extra something.

Delicious duck for gourmet cats' palates

(One portion for two feline gourmets)

- *200 g/7 oz duck breast fillet*
- *a pinch of salt*
- *a pinch of pepper*
- *1–2 Tbs butter*
- *50 ml/2 fl oz ($^1/_4$ cup) vegetable stock*
- *grated orange rind*
- *1 apple*
- *1 knob of butter*
- *1 Tbs water*
- *1 Tbs raisins*

1. Skin the duck breast fillet and season it with salt and pepper. Heat the butter in a frying pan and brown the duck breast on both sides for approximately 6 minutes. Remove the meat from the frying pan, cover and place in a slightly warm oven.

2. Add some vegetable stock to the meat juices and reduce. Flavour with a little grated rind of an untreated orange.

3. Peel and core the apple and cut it into slices. Melt the butter in a small frying pan, carefully fry the apple pieces in the fat, add some water and cook in approximately 4 to 5 minutes. Finally add the raisins.

4. Warm up the duck breast in the reduced sauce. Cut the meat into thin slices, drizzle with the sauce and serve on a plate, garnished with the apple slices.

Stuffed chicken breast fillet "Cat's dream"

(One portion for two feline gourmets)

1. Cut a pocket into the chicken breast fillet, season with salt and pepper and drizzle with lemon juice.

2. Trim and cut the fresh cep mushrooms into slices; if using dried mushrooms, soak them in warm water for about an hour and then squeeze out the water. Finely dice the shallot and boil the parsley and chervil.

3. Heat the butter in a frying pan and sauté the fresh or soaked mushrooms with the onion and herbs in the fat.

4. Place the stuffing in the pocket of the chicken breast fillet and close with a toothpick. Heat the oil in a frying pan and brown the meat thoroughly on all sides. Add the vegetable stock and simmer for approximately 15 to 20 minutes at reduced temperature. Remove the meat from the frying pan and let it settle.

5. Stir the sour cream into the meat juices and reduce. Mix the sauce with the cooked rice. Let the mixture cool down a little and place in the cat's bowl. Remove the toothpick, cut the chicken breast fillet into slices and arrange on top of the rice.

- *200 g/7 oz chicken breast fillet*
- *a pinch of salt*
- *a pinch of pepper*
- *1 tsp lemon juice*
- *3 fresh or 10 g/$^1/_3$ oz dried cep mushrooms*
- *1 shallot*
- *sprigs of parsley and chervil*
- *1 tsp butter*
- *1 Tbs oil*
- *$^1/_4$ cup vegetable stock*
- *1 Tbs sour cream*
- *50 g/2 oz ($^1/_3$ cup) boiled rice*

Meatloaf "Green meadow"

- 150 g/5 oz minced meat
- 1 egg
- 1 onion, chopped
- 1 anchovy fillet, chopped
- 1 bread roll, soaked in water
- 2 Tbs oat flakes
- salt and pepper
- 1 Tbs bread crumbs
- 1 Tbs herbs (chives, parsley), chopped
- cucumber and tomato slices for garnish

(One portion for two feline gourmets)

1. Mix the mince, egg, chopped onions and anchovies, the bread roll soaked in water and the oat flakes, a pinch of salt and pepper and knead well.

2. Shape the mixture into an oblong loaf and roll in the bread-crumbs and chopped herbs. Place the loaf into an ovenproof greased dish and put into the pre-heated oven.

3. Cook for approximately 60 minutes at 200 °C (390 °F), Gas mark 6. Remove from the dish and let the meatloaf cool down before cutting it into slices. Garnish with cucumber and tomato slices.

Liver balls "Cat's paw"

- 150 g/5 oz ox liver
- 1 Tbs butter
- 5 Tbs oat flakes
- 1 tsp oil
- 1 Tbs carrot, grated
- 1 Tbs oat flakes
- 1 Tbs chives, chopped

(One portion for two feline gourmets)

1. Fry the ox liver in butter, cut into strips and chop in the mixer. Add the oat flakes, the oil and the grated carrot and knead well.

2. Shape little balls and roll in the oat flakes and chives.

Hare fillet "Speedy González"

(One portion for two feline gourmets)

1. Cut the bacon into strips and slices. Lard the fillet with the strips, season with a little salt and pepper and wrap in the bacon slices.

2. Fry the fillet wrapped in bacon in a frying pan on all sides until it has a golden brown colour; remove and keep warm.

3. Boil the pasta in salt water al dente. Add the cider vinegar and the meat stock to the meat juices, bring quickly to the boil and reduce a little. Round off with the sour cream.

4. Cut the fillet into bite-sized pieces. Mix the pasta with the sauce and arrange together with the meat. Sprinkle with grated carrot and chopped parsley.

- *2 slices of bacon*
- *1 fillet of hare*
- *salt and pepper*
- *60 g/2 oz pasta*
- *1 tsp cider vinegar*
- *2–3 Tbs vegetable stock*
- *1 Tbs sour cream*
- *1 Tbs carrot, grated*
- *1 Tbs parsley, chopped*

Meat balls "Big turkey"

(One portion for two feline gourmets)

1. Fry the turkey breast fillet in butter, cut into fine strips and chop in the mixer.

2. Mix the chopped meat with the egg and rice and knead well. Shape into balls with moist hands. Roll in the oat flakes before serving.

- *100 g/3½ oz turkey breast fillet*
- *1 Tbs butter*
- *1 egg*
- *40 g/1½ oz (¼ cup) boiled rice*
- *1 Tbs oat flakes*

Chicken breast fillet "Tender tongue"

(One portion for two feline gourmets)

- 100 g/3½ oz chicken breast fillet
- ½ tsp three-algae powder
- 1 tsp duck lard

1. Sprinkle the chicken breast fillet with three-algae powder. Heat the duck lard in a non-stick frying pan and cook slowly so that it does not dry out.

2. Wrap the cooked meat in aluminium foil and let it rest for approximately 10 minutes, so that the juices can settle. Cut into small cubes and serve either on its own or mixed with fresh vegetables.

Note
If you don't have any duck lard available, you can replace it with oil, butter or margarine for frying.

Snow peas "Sweet snout"

(One portion for one feline gourmet)

1. Heat the oil in a frying pan and fry the snow peas. Add the cider vinegar and soy sauce, stir frequently and simmer for approximately 10 minutes.

2. Bring the salt water to the boil, sprinkle in the rice, bring to the boil again quickly and cook at reduced heat, and let the rice swell up.

3. Cut the pods into small pieces, mix with the rice and yeast flakes and serve.

- *1 tsp oil*
- *40 g/1½ oz (¼ cup) snow peas*
- *1 tsp cider vinegar*
- *1 tsp soy sauce*
- *40 g/1½ oz (¼ cup) rice*

Breast fillet of guinea fowl à la crème for gourmet cats

(One portion for two feline gourmets)

- *1 guinea fowl breast fillet*
- *1 Tbs butter*
- *1 tsp cream (15%)*
- *7–8 seaweed flakes*

1. Carefully fry the guinea fowl breast fillet in butter with the skin side down for approximately 4 minutes at a low temperature. Turn the meat and fry for 1 minute from the other side and then place in the oven pre-heated to 100°C (210°F) Gas mark 1, so that it continues to cook slowly.

2. Remove the skin with a paper towel and cut the meat into cubes. Mix with a little cream and the seaweed flakes soaked in hot water.

Asparagus tips in creamed rice

(One portion for two feline gourmets)

- *60g/2oz ($^1/_3$ cup) rice*
- *6 asparagus tips*
- *1 knob of butter*
- *a pinch of salt*
- *a pinch of sugar*

1. Sprinkle the rice into boiling salt water, bring to the boil, lower the temperature and let the rice boil and swell at a low temperature.

2. Bring the water to the boil and add a knob of butter, a pinch of salt and sugar. Let the asparagus tips simmer in the hot water for approximately 5 minutes, but do not boil.

3. Carefully mix the rice with the asparagus tips, season and serve with the creamed rice.

Crunchy fishy titbits

(One portion for two feline gourmets)

- *200 g/7 oz fresh mackerel fillet*
- *1 egg*
- *50 g/2 oz ($^1/_4$ cup) oat flakes*
- *1 tsp oil*
- *1 Tbs grated Parmesan cheese*
- *1 Tbs chopped parsley*

Note
Cats will not turn their noses up at breadcrumbs if you use them instead of oat flakes.

1. Roll the fresh mackerel fillet in the beaten egg. Put the oat flakes in a little bowl and coat the fish with the flakes.

2. Heat the oil in a frying pan and brown the fish briefly on both sides. Reduce the temperature and let the fish cook at a medium temperature on both sides for approximately 15 minutes.

3. Let the fish cool down and break up into bite-sized pieces. Mix grated cheese and chopped parsley and sprinkle over the crunchy titbits.

Ragout of sardines "Fresh breeze"

- *1 carrot*
- *2 sardines in oil*
- *$^1/_2$ Tbs yeast flakes*
- *1 tsp cider vinegar*
- *1 tsp sour cream*
- *flat-leaf parsley*

(One portion for two feline gourmets)

1. Trim and slice a small carrot and cook in a little salt water. Drain the carrots and let them cool down a little.

2. Chop the sardines and mix with the carrot slices, yeast flakes and cider vinegar. Arrange on a plate and garnish with a dollop of sour cream and flat-leaf parsley.

"Happy cat" cheese omelette with bacon

(One portion for one feline gourmet)

1. Whisk the egg with cat milk. Heat the oil in a frying pan. Pour the egg mixture in slowly, making sure that it does not stick.

2. Place the grated cheese and the bacon cubes into the middle. Once the mixture has thickened, carefully fold over and turn. Cook until golden yellow on both sides.

3. Let the omelette cool down a little, cut into bite-sized pieces and sprinkle with freshly chopped herbs such as chives and parsley.

- *1 egg*
- *3 Tbs cat milk*
- *1 tsp oil*
- *1 Tbs grated Swiss cheese*
- *1 Tbs bacon, cut into cubes*
- *1 Tbs chives, chopped into rings*
- *1 Tbs parsley, chopped*

Tomcat Charlie's cheese balls

- 200g/7oz (1½ cups) grated Emmental cheese or Swiss cheese
- 50g/2oz yoghurt
- 80g/3oz (½ cup) cooked rice or oat flakes
- 50g/2oz (½ stick) low-fat margarine
- 2 Tbs grated hazelnuts or coconut

(One portion for two feline gourmets)

1. Mix the grated Emmental cheese well with the yoghurt and oat flakes or rice and the low-fat margarine.

2. Shape the mixture into little balls. Put the grated hazelnuts or coconut into a little bowl and toss the balls in the bowl to coat.

Egg flakes with mixed herbs

- 2 eggs
- 2 Tbs water
- 2 Tbs cat milk
- 1 Tbs parsley, chopped
- 1 Tbs dill
- 2 tsp oil
- a few drops of soy sauce
- 1–2 tsp tomato paste

(One portion for two feline gourmets)

1. Whisk the eggs with water and milk and stir in the herb mixture.

2. Heat the oil in the frying pan and slowly pour in the mixture. Stir with a wooden spoon and push the flakes that form together in the middle of the frying pan until all the liquid has thickened.

3. Let the fluffy scrambled egg cool down a little, drizzle with a few drops of soy sauce and garnish with a little tomato paste before serving.

Note
To keep the scrambled eggs soft, thicken the egg mixture at a low temperature.

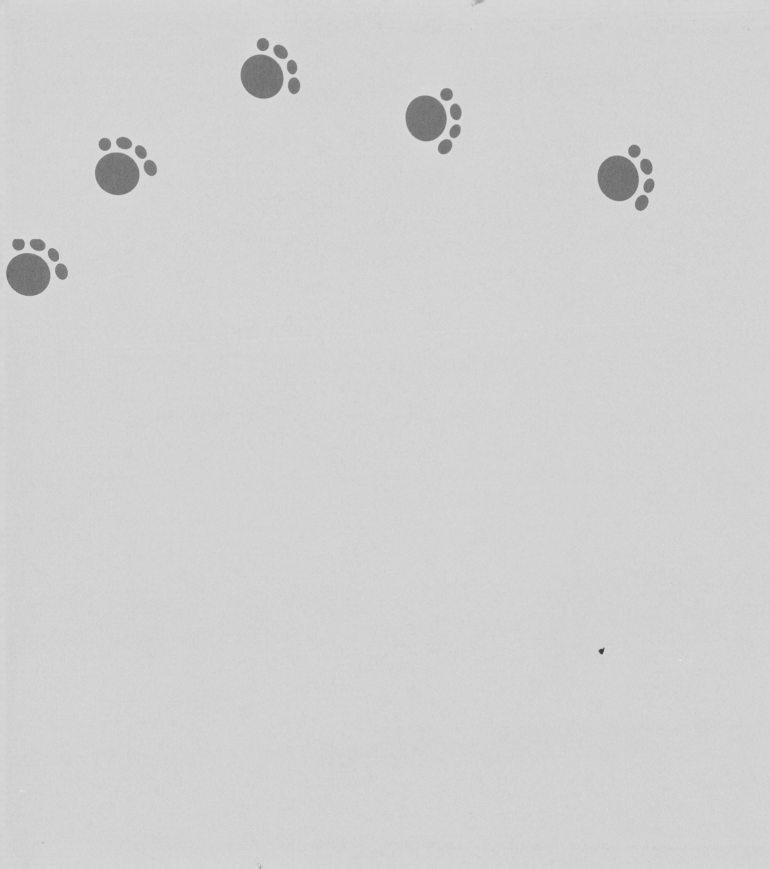